Testing with Models

Robin Johnson

CRABTREE
PUBLISHING COMPANY
WWW.CRABTREEBOOKS.COM

Title-Specific Learning Objectives:

Readers will:

- Identify the reasons the author gives to explain why testing models is very important to engineers.
- Describe different types of models, including drawings, diagrams, and models with moving parts.
- Explain how models help engineers find the best solutions.

High-frequency words (grade one) a, are, can, have, how, this, we, with, you	Academic vocabulary artificial, blueprint, creative thinking, diagram, drawing, energy, materials, robot, wind turbine

Before, During, and After Reading Prompts:

Activate Prior Knowledge and Make Predictions:

Have children read the title of the book and look at the cover image and the image on the title page. Discuss their thoughts on the following questions:

- What is a model? What are they used for? Who uses them?
- What are the models on the front cover like?
- What model do you see on the title page? How is it different from the models on the front cover?

During Reading:

After reading page 11, draw children's attention to the images. Ask them to consider how the two different models show the same thing in different ways. Ask prompting questions such as:

- How are the models different? How are they similar? What parts of a mountain does each model show? Which model works better?

After Reading:

Have children make a list of the different types of models mentioned in the book. On an anchor chart, write down two characteristics of each type of model.

Have children reflect on why it is important to test models of different solutions. Add "Reasons to Test Models" to the anchor chart.

Author: Robin Johnson

Series Development: Reagan Miller

Editor: Janine Deschenes

Proofreader: Melissa Boyce

STEAM Notes for Educators: Janine Deschenes

Guided Reading Leveling: Publishing Solutions Group

Cover, Interior Design, and Prepress: Samara Parent

Photo research: Robin Johnson and Samara Parent

Production coordinator: Katherine Berti

Photographs:
Alamy: Sergey Nivens: p. 8
Getty: Mark Gail/The Washington Post: p. 9
iStock: Steve Debenport: cover
Shutterstock: Lano Lan: p. 7 (t)
All other photographs by Shutterstock

Library and Archives Canada Cataloguing in Publication

Title: Testing with models / Robin Johnson.
Names: Johnson, Robin (Robin R.), author.
Description: Series statement: Full STEAM ahead! | Includes index.
Identifiers: Canadiana (print) 20190133694 |
  Canadiana (ebook) 20190133724 |
  ISBN 9780778764588 (softcover) |
  ISBN 9780778764083 (hardcover) |
  ISBN 9781427123602 (HTML)
Subjects: LCSH: Engineering models—Juvenile literature. |
  LCSH: Models and modelmaking—Juvenile
  literature. | LCSH: Engineering—Juvenile literature.
Classification: LCC TA177 .J64 2019 | DDC j620.001/1—dc23

Library of Congress Cataloging-in-Publication Data

Names: Johnson, Robin (Robin R.), author.
Title: Testing with models / Robin Johnson.
Description: New York, New York : Crabtree Publishing Company,
  [2020] | Series: Full STEAM ahead! | Includes index.
Identifiers: LCCN 2019025168 (print) | LCCN 2019025169 (ebook) |
  ISBN 9780778764083 (hardcover) |
  ISBN 9780778764588 (paperback) |
  ISBN 9781427123602 (ebook)
Subjects: LCSH: Engineering models--Juvenile literature.
Classification: LCC TA177 .J64 2020 (print) | LCC TA177 (ebook) |
  DDC 620/.0044-dc23
LC record available at https://lccn.loc.gov/2019025168
LC ebook record available at https://lccn.loc.gov/2019025169

Printed in the U.S.A./102019/CG20190809

Table of Contents

Crabtree Publishing Company
www.crabtreebooks.com   1-800-387-7650

Published in Canada
Crabtree Publishing
616 Welland Ave.
St. Catharines, Ontario
L2M 5V6

Published in the United States
Crabtree Publishing
PMB 59051
350 Fifth Avenue, 59th Floor
New York, New York 10118

Published in the United Kingdom
Crabtree Publishing
Maritime House
Basin Road North, Hove
BN41 1WR

Published in Australia
Crabtree Publishing
Unit 3 – 5 Currumbin Court
Capalaba
QLD 4157

What is a Model?

Have you ever played with a dollhouse or a toy car? They are both models. A model is a **representation** of a real object. That means a model can stand in place of something else.

Models are often smaller than the real objects.

Some models are fun to play with!

We can't visit planets—but we can make models to see them up close!

5

Models Help Us Learn

We can use models to help us learn. Models show us how things look and how they work. They show us the different parts of an object.

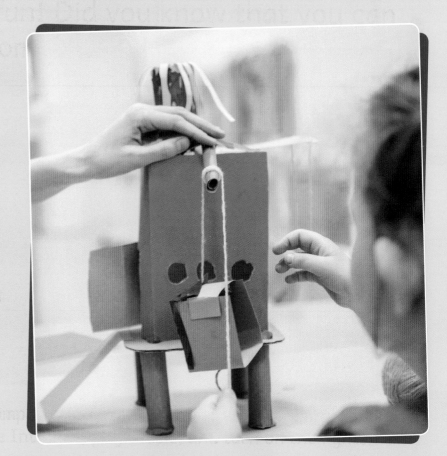

This student made a model of a building. She sees how the parts, such as the roof and the walls, fit together.

These students are using a model to see how a toy car works.

This boy is using a globe to find the countries around the world. A globe is a model of Earth.

Engineers Use Models

Models help engineers learn too! Engineers are people who use math, science, and **creative thinking** to solve problems. Making and testing models are important parts of solving problems.

Bridges solve the problem of crossing over water. Before an engineer builds a bridge, they make a model to plan how it will look and work.

Engineers test models to make sure they work well. This bridge model did not pass the test! The engineer will fix the model and test it again.

Many Models

There are many types of models. Some models are objects with different shapes and **materials**. Other models are drawings. We can use different types of models to represent the same thing.

Many models are made on computers.

These kids are making a model of a mountain. It is an object made of different shapes and materials. It shows what a mountain looks like.

This drawing is a model too. It shows where real mountains and trees are found in an area.

All the Same

All models are the same in some ways. Models show how real things look or work. They show how parts fit together. Models also show areas that can be improved, or made better.

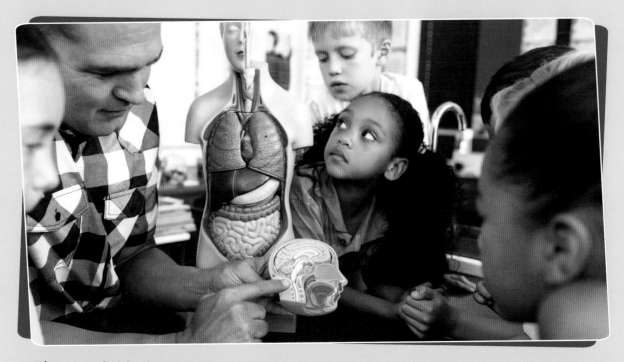

This model helps students learn what the parts of the human body look like. It also helps them understand how the parts fit together.

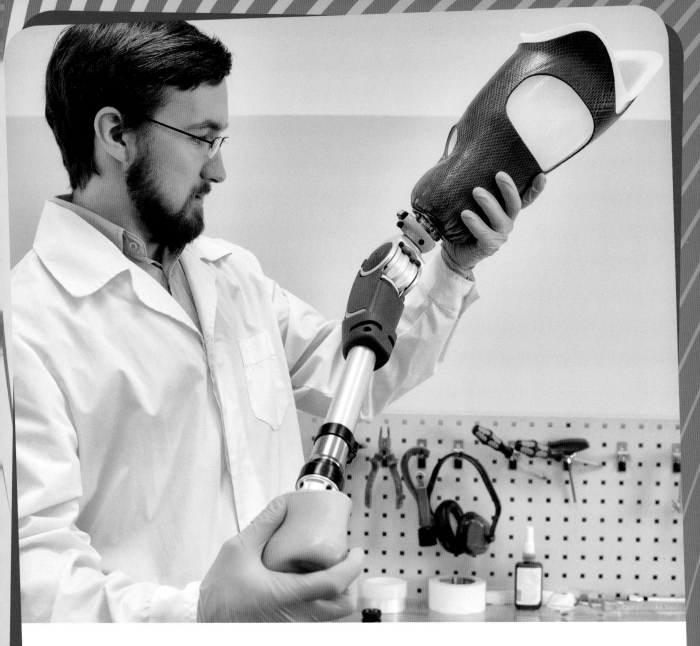

This engineer is using a model to make an **artificial** leg.
He will test the leg to see how it works. The test will show
if any parts need to be improved.

Spot the Differences

Models are also different in some ways. Drawings and **diagrams** may have labels that name or explain parts. Other models may have parts that move.

This diagram shows how we can get **energy** from the wind.

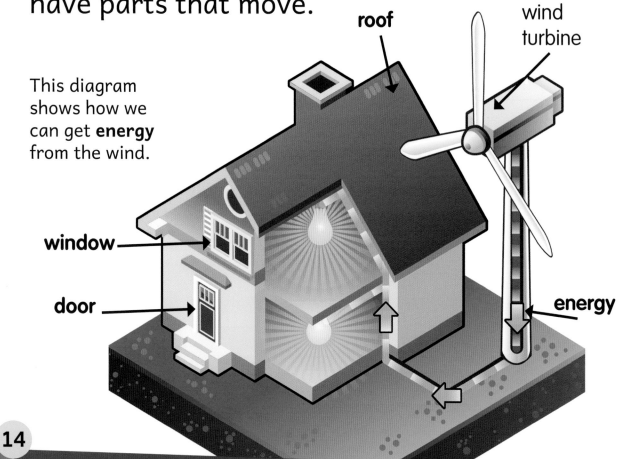

roof

wind turbine

window

door

energy

This model shows how we can get energy from the wind too.
It has parts that move. It shows how parts of a wind turbine spin
when the wind blows.

Models are Tools

Models are important tools for engineers. Engineers use models to make plans. They use models to test their **designs**. They also use models to show and explain their ideas.

Tools are things that help us do jobs. Engineers need models to do their job.

This engineer is sharing a blueprint with others. A blueprint is a model that shows the parts of a building.

These engineers are using a model to plan a tall building.

Robot Redo

A team of engineers wanted to make a robot that walks. They used models to plan and test their designs. They picked the best model. Then they improved it.

Engineers used diagrams to help plan their robot.

The engineers tested this model to make sure it moved well.

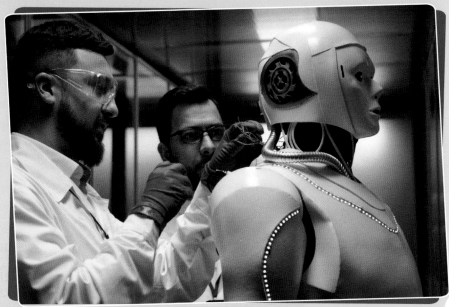

The engineers found a problem and fixed the model.

19

Designs for Fun

Another team of engineers wanted to make a new playground. They used models to test different designs, shapes, and materials.

The engineers used drawings to plan the design of the playground.

Engineers design playgrounds with strong, safe materials.
Engineers work hard so we can have fun!

Words to Know

artificial [ahr-tuh-FISH-uhl] adjective Made by humans

creative thinking [kree-EY-tiv THING-king] noun Using your mind to make up new and original ideas

design [dih-ZAHYN] noun The first models or drawings of something

diagrams [DAHY-uh-grams] noun Drawings that show an object's parts and how it works

energy [EN-er-jee] noun The power to do work

materials [muh-TEER-ee-uhls] noun Things from which something is made

representation [rep-ri-zen-TEY-shuh n] noun Something that looks like or stands in for a real object

wind turbine [wind TUR-bahyn] noun A machine that is moved by the wind and that creates energy

A noun is a person, place, or thing.

A verb is an action word that tells you what someone or something does.

An adjective is a word that tells you what something is like.

Index

About the Author

Robin Johnson is a freelance author and editor who has written more than 80 children's books. When she isn't working, Robin builds castles in the sky with her engineer husband and their two best creations—sons Jeremy and Drew.

To explore and learn more, enter the code at the Crabtree Plus website below.

www.crabtreeplus.com/fullsteamahead

Your code is:
fsa20

STEAM Notes for Educators

Full STEAM Ahead is a literacy series that helps readers build vocabulary, fluency, and comprehension while learning about big ideas in STEAM subjects. *Testing with Models* helps readers learn to identify the reasons an author gives to support their points. Readers will identify how the author supports the idea that testing models is important to engineers. The STEAM activity below helps readers extend the ideas in the book to build their skills in engineering, arts, and technology.

Exploring Types of Models

Children will be able to:
- Create two different models that show the same solution.
- Test the models and use video to document the testing process.

Materials
- Model Worksheet
- Device that can record video

Guiding Prompts
After reading *Testing with Models*, ask children:
- What is a model?
- Why do engineers use models? How do models help them find solutions?
- Can you name some of the types of models mentioned in this book?

Activity Prompts
Explain to children that they will create different types of models that will show a class-generated solution. First, pose a scenario to children. Use the following scenario, or work with any themes that are already being discussed in class.
- Jane brings her lunches to school in a lunch box. But every time she opens it at lunchtime, her juice box has squished her sandwich! Help Jane design a solution.

Split children into groups. Each group brainstorms possible solutions to the problem and chooses their best solution. Guide children through this step. Next, hand each group the Model Worksheet. Each group must create a model on paper (a drawing or a diagram) and a physical model (one with or without moving parts) that shows their solution.

Use the video recording device to record each group presenting their drawing or diagram, and testing their physical model. Ask each group how each model helps them share the solution with others. Do some models work well for certain purposes? Have a viewing day in which children watch the videos and discuss which solutions worked best.

Extensions
- Invite children to document, using photos or video, other solutions to problems. Create a class blog to share solutions with other young engineers.

To view and download the worksheet, visit **www.crabtreebooks.com/resources/ printables** or **www.crabtreeplus.com/ fullsteamahead** and enter the code **fsa20**.